Abe

We have come a
long way together
my friend...
long may it
continue yet :)

WHAT JESUS WAS REALLY SAYING

how we turned his
teachings upside down

IAN LAWTON

Rational Spirituality Press **RSP**

First published in 2016 by Rational Spirituality Press.
All enquiries to be directed to www.rspress.org.

Copyright © Ian Lawton 2016. All rights reserved.

The rights of Ian Lawton to be identified as the Author of the Work have been asserted by him in accordance with the Copyright, Designs and Patents Act 1988.

No part of this book may be used or reproduced in any manner whatsoever (excluding brief quotations embodied in critical articles and reviews), nor by way of trade or otherwise be lent, resold, hired out, or otherwise circulated in any form of binding or cover other than that in which it is published, without the publisher's prior written consent.

All biblical quotes come from the New Revised Standard Version (see www.devotions.net/bible/00new.htm)

A CIP catalogue record for this title is available from the British Library.

ISBN 978-0-9928163-1-5

Cover photo and design by Ian Lawton.
Author photograph by Simon Howson-Green.

each of us is a god	2
the nature of reality	10
the truth about the Bible	29
they weren't miracles	54
faith can move mountains	74
there are no victims	92
the past is the past	109
the law of attraction	114
anyone can do what he did	122
being the light	130

each of us

is a god

WHAT JESUS WAS REALLY SAYING

> 'I tell you, the one who believes in me will also do the works that I do and, in fact, will do greater works than these.' (John 14:12)

Is it really possible that no Christian scholar has ever understood the true meaning, indeed the enormous power, of this statement?

Is it really possible that this and selected other quotations that still survive, scattered amongst the four gospels of the New Testament, are echoes of messages that had become seriously distorted and misunderstood within only a few generations of Jesus' death?

Is it really possible that these echoes have had to wait until such time as various scientific and other developments could properly illuminate them – thereby restoring Jesus' true, original messages in all their majesty?

This book will contend that the answer

WHAT JESUS WAS REALLY SAYING

to all these questions may well be 'yes'.

In recent decades many secular researchers have applied themselves to seeing through the distortions in the Bible. They have fascinated us with stories about Jesus' supposed bloodline, or about the holy grail that supposedly once contained his blood. Perhaps most important so far, they've suggested that Mary Magdalene may not only have been his lover but also very much his equal in what was a truly revolutionary movement — and in doing so they've exposed the potential manipulation of a patriarchal Church that may have suppressed this truth for millennia to serve their own political ends.

But it's entirely possible that all this has really just been a series of sideshows waiting for the main event — a complete reinterpretation, arguably indeed a restoration, of Jesus' fundamental messages for humanity.

There is one major difference between this modern presentation of his messages and the way in which they were originally given to us – this time there is no one who can be worshipped. Although as we'll see it was essential that Jesus incarnated in the physical world as a human being to give us practical demonstrations of just what we're capable of, in hindsight the downside was that back then the people he was dealing with simply weren't ready to worship *themselves* in their *own* magnificence – so they naturally worshipped him instead.

It seems that the many millions of people to whom the Christian message has spread in the intervening millennia have been no more ready. But perhaps now, in a less religiously controlled world that allows more freedom of thought, conditions are ~~more~~ ripe — at least for seeds to be planted that may, eventually, blossom into an entirely different future.

These restored messages are sufficiently powerful that they *could* usher in a whole new era in human development and evolution. They *could* allow us to finally break away from all our superstitions about Jesus and the countless other gods and prophets we've invented or misunderstood — ever since we first started to recognise our mortality as physical beings and to wonder 'what lies beyond'.

This is a chance for each of us to be empowered as individuals — for each of us to take responsibility for our own life experience, and to recognise that we ourselves are creating it. But, if enough of us wake up this time, it's also a chance for the human race as a whole to leave childish things behind and to finally mature into collective adulthood.

This may sound a little harsh, but all the evidence suggests that we're still so far from a true understanding of who and what we really are that only strong words will awaken those who are ready from their slumber.

Of course many won't be ready yet, and that's fine. We just need to make a start. Indeed the ball has already been rolling for some time, thanks to the many books and films about 'positive thinking', the 'law of attraction' and so on that have proved extremely popular in recent decades. Some may have contained a somewhat limited, even somewhat distorted, perspective, but they have nonetheless sowed hugely important seeds.

So conditions may now be ripe for a new and powerful understanding to spread until at some point it becomes unstoppable. And what lies at the heart of this new understanding?

The only difference between us and Jesus is that he knew he was divine, whereas we've yet to realise that we are too.

That's it. So simple. So concise. But are we really ready to take that message on board?

One reason some people have struggled with this is that they have a confused view of what being 'divine' means, so let's clarify this right from the outset. At its simplest it means *knowing* that as human beings we're not minnows swimming around hopelessly and helplessly in a huge pond of someone else's making, but instead are completely in charge of the illusion we call physical life on planet earth. It means *knowing* that, subject to just a few limitations, each of us is creating every single experience we're having. No one else. Just us.

Of course many people believe that our real aim on this planet is to pursue an often complex and long drawn out path towards 'enlightenment' or 'ascension'. But if this reinterpretation-cum-restoration of Jesus' messages is accurate, it's a pretty good bet he would adopt a quite different stance:

Simply recognising that we're the master of our own creation is all we need to do to reconnect with our true divinity.

the nature of reality

WHAT JESUS WAS REALLY SAYING

We can't understand who we really are unless we have a proper grasp of the nature of the reality we've chosen to inhabit. The assertion that follows may seem counter-intuitive, but it's none the less true for that:

In order to understand the reality we live in, first we need to understand the realities we'll experience after we die.

In Jesus' lifetime what passed for ideas about what happens after death were mostly superstitious nonsense. The situation isn't necessarily much better now. But at least in our modern world we have access to the hugely important research of a significant number of consciousness explorers who've learned to deliberately take themselves 'out of body', or OOB. We might note that this common description isn't really accurate, because often these experienced researchers aren't actually 'travelling' anywhere external to themselves – it's more that they access other planes of consciousness by 'going within'. In any case the plethora of convincing evidence their brave and pioneering work has placed before us should make it much easier for us to finally understand Jesus' true messages.[1]

What they've been describing for some decades, many in books that are still readily available, is that we can access what we think of as the afterlife realms right now – while we're still alive – and explore them as much as we like.

What they've also been telling us is that this reality we're experiencing is not as 'real' as we think it is. Or, looking at it another way, there are a great many

---

[1] I discuss all this research and evidence, with copious quotations and source references, in my book *Afterlife*.

realities that are all different – but just as real to the consciousnesses experiencing them as ours is to us. What is more many of them are less 'physical' – although again that's not strictly accurate, because to their mostly unenlightened inhabitants they're just as physical as our reality appears to us. So perhaps we'll call them 'less energetically dense' realms, or realms of 'higher vibration', instead.

Most important for our current purposes, these OOB explorers have all come to realise pretty swiftly that, in these other realms, their expectations, intentions, thoughts and emotions control everything that happens. To understand this better, let's look at some examples of what they've discovered about behaviour therein.

They've found that some people die so suddenly they don't even know they're dead, and literally carry on as before in the same earthly surroundings – although somewhat confused to find that other people don't see or talk to them, and that the rules have changed because they can walk through walls and so on.

They've also discovered that others who die suddenly *do* realise what's happened but cling to the earth experience. Some do this because they simply can't imagine there's anywhere else to go. But others are dominated by the impulse to, for example, take revenge on their murderer, or on a cheating partner; or to complete unfinished projects they think are important; or to try to communicate, usually in vain, with their loved ones – although we might also note that those left behind often exert such a strong energetic pull on the departed, with their intense emotions of loss, that they prevent them from properly moving on.

Others still attach themselves to people who are still alive because they crave the experience of alcohol or drugs, or whatever they themselves were addicted to. Or they can be attracted to someone whose predominant emotion – say anger or lust – matches how they were themselves. In these cases they're trying to get their 'fix' second-hand. But we should be clear that most of these 'spirit attachments' are pretty harmless.

All this means that the ideas we've developed about ghosts and so on aren't so very far off. It's just that most of us fail to realise that this is a widespread experience, affecting a great many departed souls who have become so immersed in the illusion of life on earth that they can't leave.

In fact OOB explorers have repeatedly reported that, with an ever-expanding human population, there's now a huge build-up of souls trapped in what we might call the 'near-earth' plane. What is more many of these explorers spend a great deal of time working with entities from the higher realms trying to help those who are trapped to move on. Nevertheless free-will always prevails, so those who are really insistent on staying stuck will do exactly that. They may even be so wrapped up in their own personal hell of recrimination and self-loathing, and of replaying earthly events over and over again, that they don't even notice there's anyone trying to help them.

In just the same way human explorers pretty quickly realise just how much their thoughts and so on control their experience when their consciousness is no longer restricted to their physical body. Often in their early forays they only have to think briefly about the body they appear to have left behind and zap! they're straight back in it again. Or, if they stay in the near-earth plane, sometimes they only have to think of a friend or location and zap! they're immediately there.

Even more important for the messages Jesus was trying to teach, once they start exploring realms of even slightly higher vibration they find their thoughts influence their entire environment. What is more that's exactly how it works for people who die and leave our world for good. If they're not bogged down with heavy negative emotions, and they're ready for the 'transition', and they believe in some sort of heavenly afterlife, then they'll experience whatever they conceive that to be.

If it's a crystal castle on a high snow-capped mountain, then that's exactly the environment they find themselves in; or a green meadow full of wild flowers; a beach with pure white sand; a little shack in the wilderness; an Egyptian temple; the possibilities are endless. But these may be merely temporary and predominantly individual experiences before they move on to something else.

By contrast there are also what modern explorers call 'consensus realities', which are more permanent and can involve significant numbers of souls. Some of the finest examples of these are the religion-based heavens or hells. Yes, these really *do* exist – and there are as many of them as there have been religions, and different strains of those religions.

If someone is a fervent member of a particular Christian denomination, for example, a host of their predecessors have already created the heavenly version of it purely with their thoughts and expectations – and after death that person may well find themselves going to church and practising exactly the same rituals as before. Many OOB explorers have documented these scenarios in startlingly similar ways.

Effectively each of these realities is just another illusion. So we'd all do well to prepare ourselves for the afterlife by understanding that, while *anything* and *everything* is possible, almost all of it is just another illusion we can move on from. What is more there's no ultimate destination – or at least the afterlife journey never stops, as far as we can tell so far.

The other important thing OOB explorers have learned about these consensus realities is that their own thoughts have far less influence there – because the greater the number of souls contributing to a given experience, especially with shared expectations, the harder it is for any one of them or someone from outside to significantly alter it.

WHAT JESUS WAS REALLY SAYING

This fact in particular has a significant bearing on the experience we're having now in the earth plane.

The first thing we need to understand about our own reality of life on earth is that it operates at a relatively low level of vibration — so our thoughts and expectations don't influence it with anything like the rapidity of some of the higher vibratory planes. There's a significant time delay. Indeed space-time itself is much more prevalent in our reality than in many others — which is why, when we're immersed in it, we can't travel at the 'speed of thought' as in higher realms unless we significantly alter our state of consciousness.

Ours is also very much a consensus reality. This adds to the delays in seeing our thoughts feed through into our experience, because they have to be processed alongside all the myriad, often conflicting, thoughts of the other people who have an influence on that bit of our shared reality, whatever it is.

Sport provides us with a wonderful example of this. Sports psychology is big business in our modern world. So, apart from the physical training, the honing of skills and so on, the greater the mental focus a sportsperson puts into their desired outcome – an Olympic gold medal or whatever – the greater their chance of achieving it.

They do this partly by using their *thoughts* and *imagination* – that is by visualising the desired outcome happening – and partly by setting up a hugely intense *expectation* of success, and maintaining that intensity for a long time. Of course because in sport there's always more than one person competing for the prize, the one who does all this better than the others on any given day wins. That's an excellent demonstration of how a shared or consensus reality works.

But even if we can accept that our intentions, thoughts and expectations have this much effect when we're focussing them on a particular outcome we desire, we still have to ask ourselves what's happening the rest of the time – in our everyday lives when undesirable thing happen, or when we strive for something but fail? Some people simply say all the rest is blind chance, others that some things just aren't meant to be, others that it is or isn't God's will. Others still claim it's their karma from past lives, or something that wasn't on their life plan.

But is any of that really logical? Let's think about this carefully for a moment:

If we accept that it's possible to create desirable outcomes in our life, why would

WHAT JESUS WAS REALLY SAYING

we then insist on blaming something or someone else for our less desirable experiences?

Where's the sense or consistency in that? Doesn't it make far more sense just to accept that we're creating the *entirety* of our experience, not just via our proactive thoughts and intentions but also via our *underlying* beliefs, preconceptions and attitudes – indeed via everything that forms part of our psychological, mental and emotional make up, both conscious and unconscious?

Because ours is a consensus reality it operates according to a set of rules we've built up over time, based on our experiences. Nowhere is this more in evidence than in the fact that objects and people *appear* physical to us. Actually our brains and accompanying senses and organs have evolved to be hard-wired to perceive them as such.

So we simply don't believe we can pass our hand straight through a table.

But we can. *I still can't accept this!*

If that's just too big as an initial conceptual step, think of the well-known anecdotes of desperate mothers lifting heavy cars to rescue their trapped child. Are they obeying the normal laws of physics as we commonly understand them when they do that? Of course not. The intensity of their emotion, of their desire and, above all, of their *belief* that they can and must save their child, produces a momentary suspension of those laws.

Such a feat can be achieved by anyone at any time, as long as they have the requisite belief – and this book contends that *that's* what Jesus was trying to tell and show us.

WHAT JESUS WAS REALLY SAYING

Recognition that the reality we inhabit is actually in large part an illusion should not be mistaken for criticism of our way of life or of the consensus reality we've developed. Our earth plane is an extremely useful environment in which to gather experience – which is all consciousness ever wants to do.

We'll delve more into ultimate aims and the truly big picture later, but for now the point to appreciate is that the reality we've chosen to experience is an *extremely* persuasive illusion. Yet being able to see it as such, even if only to a relatively limited extent, can significantly enhance our experience of it – and make it a lot less painful too.

If we stand back and look at ourselves it should be pretty obvious that, as humans, many of us are addicted to suffering. But the 'good news' Jesus was trying to bring us is that we don't *have* to suffer. In truth we *all* have the capability to shape our human experience into *whatever* we want it to be, subject to a few constraints that we'll discuss shortly. But even if we don't create the *perfect* life for ourselves – whatever that might be – and only manage to influence our experience to a more limited extent, that's still a huge improvement over feeling we're constantly being buffeted by outrageous fortune; or that we're at the mercy of our karma, or of a God who is at best unpredictable, and at worst downright spiteful.

It's perfectly reasonable to have doubts about all this, especially on first exposure to what can seem extremely radical ideas. But we shouldn't forget that even modern scientists are having to massively broaden their view of what constitutes reality – and are increasingly having to enter the realms of *meta*physics to do it.

WHAT JESUS WAS REALLY SAYING

Their work at the quantum level indicates that dimensionality is probably much more complex than the three of space and one of time we're used to perceiving. Also that what appears to be physical matter is, at least in one sense, not physical at all – it's just energy fields vibrating at different rates. In simpler terms they'll tell you that the vast majority of any atom is just empty space.

So what would happen if someone came along and proved beyond all doubt that our apparently physical reality is just another illusion that can be manipulated at will?

What if this is what Jesus himself was doing? What if he deliberately incarnated as a human being and performed apparent miracles so that he could actually *show* us what each of us is capable of too?

We didn't get it then.

WHAT JESUS WAS REALLY SAYING

Perhaps we'll get it now if, armed with modern OOB and scientific research, we revisit messages that we may have completely misunderstand for two thousand years – turning them, quite literally, upside down.

the truth about
the Bible

WHAT JESUS WAS REALLY SAYING

If we're going to explore the echoes of Jesus' original messages by revisiting various passages from the four gospels of the New Testament, which of the multitude of versions should we use? In order to keep this book as simple as possible we'll opt for one of the most respected modern English translations, because it uses contemporary language.

Does this introduce inaccuracies? Perhaps. Worse still what if, in the quotes that follow, segments are sometimes left out in the middle of passages – as shown by ellipses – in order to shorten them by omitting irrelevant or repetitive elements, or even because otherwise they're just downright confusing or contradictory? After all, haven't Biblical scholars spent tens of thousands of hours poring over the exact meaning of each word? Just as scholars of the Koran and other holy books do?

WHAT JESUS WAS REALLY SAYING

In truth there's a serious problem with being unduly protective about any version of the Bible, or about the exact wording of particular passages – and it's one we must face head on before we go any further. The fact is that there *cannot be* any definitive version of any of this purported 'holy scripture'.

To illustrate this point, it's commonly understood that the first versions of what would become the Old Testament were pieced together from a variety of manuscripts long before Jesus' life even began, forming the sacred canon of the early Jewish religion.

But it's perhaps less well known that much of the material in the early chapters of Genesis – for example covering the creation, and the flood and its hero Noah – has now been clearly shown to have derived from similar but substantially different Mesopotamian traditions inscribed on clay tablets more than two thousand years beforehand. What is more the lists of pre- and post-flood patriarchs in those early chapters act as counterparts to the 'King Lists' found in early Chinese, Mesopotamian and Egyptian manuscripts. The aim of all these was purely political – each civilisation wanted to show that *their* lineage was the most ancient.

As far as the New Testament is concerned – and particularly the four gospels – major distortions of the events in Jesus' life had almost certainly already occurred even when the very first manuscripts were prepared some time after his death. This is reflected in the fact that the four gospels show some marked and serious discrepancies – not least in that the order of key events, or the details thereof, are often significantly different in the different accounts, or in some are completely missing. This hardly inspires confidence that any serious reliance can be placed on the detail.

Not only that but, a good while later on, a series of Church councils formalised the process of selecting which versions of which books should be incorporated in the biblical sacred canon. Admittedly this was a difficult job, but any group facing that kind of undertaking is going to have some sort of agenda – and we have strong reason to suppose that theirs had already departed significantly from Jesus' own.

As an example, nowhere did the political motivations behind the editing of supposed scripture come into play more than with the ideas of hell and of the devil. This opens up a whole new debate concerning traditional religious ideas that we'll discuss at some length over the rest of this chapter. It might seem at times that we're heading off at a tangent. However a proper discussion of these ideas is the only way to provide the crucial context needed for the reestablishment of Jesus' true messages, which will follow.

We saw in the previous chapter that OOB explorers have established that ideas of heaven and hell have no other origin than in our own imaginations and expectations, which have created a whole variety of them over time. Hell in particular only exists as an experience created by those departed souls who so completely believe they're evil and beyond redemption – or are so full of remorse for things they've done – that they punish *themselves*.

There is no objective hellish realm that awaits those who apparently do wrong – which of course means there's no devil who rules over such an empire, tempting weak people into his domain and dreaming up ever more shocking punishments for human miscreants. What is more Jesus himself almost certainly never spoke about such things.

Of course it's almost certainly the case that human beings have been having near-death and OOB experiences ever since we became sophisticated enough to remember and analyse them. So in Jesus' time any uninitiated unfortunates who tuned into what would've *appeared* to be objective hellish realms would've brought back reports that fuelled the notion. Indeed such mistakes have been made ever since, and are still made now by those not conversant with the modern body of OOB evidence.

But there's also a general consensus among secular scholars that the extension of this idea into the concepts of the devil and of eternal damnation were introduced by an early Church who understood all too well that people who are scared can be controlled. It is a technique still used very successfully by many of our governments today. At the heart of all this is usually a desire to hold onto, indeed amass, ever more power over others – and, of course, money.

All this in turn means there's no such thing as 'evil' either. This is a really difficult concept for many people to take on board, so it needs some explaining.

The first thing we should understand about concepts of good and evil is that, as a divine being, what we might call our 'true soul consciousness' knows that our human experience can best be compared to that of an actor in a play – where what happens to the character doesn't affect the actor themselves. The problem is that once we're playing our human role we tend to get so incredibly caught up in it that we forget who we really are, and allow it to cause us all sorts of pain and suffering. But we can *choose* to see it for what it is – and even to *change* the play or the scene if we don't like it.

What we also do as humans is develop all sorts of moral codes and judgments. Of course any group of people large or small has to agree a certain set of rules that allow everyone to live together in some sort of harmony. But let's not fool ourselves that there's any objectivity in all this. Each of our main religions has its own moral code and, although there are certain general similarities, in many respects they're substantially different.

Yet they can't all be right, can they? The truth is there's no *objective* right or wrong, there's *only* the moral judgments we humans choose to adopt in any given time, place and cultural setting.

Perhaps the most important piece of this

jigsaw for us to understand is the one briefly touched on earlier:

Our true soul consciousness is interested in one thing, and one thing alone: to expand itself through different experiences.

What is more *everything* that happens in our world is a valid addition to the databank of experience. This means that no judgment is attached to *any* of it at the true soul level because, at the end of the day, no *permanent* damage is done to the actors in the play. Our underlying energy or consciousness can never be destroyed, or even harmed.

This doesn't mean that as humans we don't need rules to live by, because without them we would descend into anarchy. Most obviously, most modern societies regard murder as a major crime that carries a heavy punishment. But it wasn't always that way – in the

WHAT JESUS WAS REALLY SAYING

American 'Wild West' for example. So we would do well to learn that any rules a society collectively decides to live by are nothing more than a convenience. They have no objectivity; there's no definitive moral code; and there's certainly no such thing as inherent or pure evil.

Nevertheless one major motivation does exist in our reality as a fundamental rule. Ours is often described as a 'dualistic' environment because it involves contrasts or apparent polarities. It's clearly naïve to think of these as merely 'good versus evil', or even 'good versus bad'. Some people try to take the element of judgment out and talk more in terms of 'positive versus negative', but even that doesn't really get to the heart of the duality.

What *does* is the understanding that, as human beings, we have a primary level of choice. Every single time we react to a circumstance or person, or make a decision, we choose the path of *love* or the path of *fear*. In some of the higher realms there's no duality so love is a given, but in ours taking the loving option is always a *choice*.

Practical examples of fear-based reactions and emotions include worry, pessimism, fear of losing possessions or love, judgment of others, impatience, greed, guilt and unkindness – and, at their worst, hatred, bitterness, revenge and so on. The love-based ones, on the other hand, include optimism, calmness, patience, forgiveness, empathy, kindness, selflessness, generosity and humour. The much publicised concept of living in the present or 'in the now' rather than in the past or future tends to foster a love-based approach to life too.

So how does this fit with the primary

universal motivation of consciousness always wanting to expand itself via experience, irrespective of what that experience is? The answer is that, in our dualistic reality, any loving response will tend to produce far more of an expansion of consciousness than a fear-based one – and, except in a very few extreme cases, will literally make us *feel* far better. For the vast majority of people this is an inherent part of our human programming.

Admittedly some individuals are born into circumstances so far removed from love that they struggle to experience or project it ever, in any form at all – and these are the ones some people would call 'evil'. But we should recognise by now that this is just another judgment.

How do we know how we'd react if we'd been born into their environment, and been through what they went through?

WHAT JESUS WAS REALLY SAYING

Of course we've all seen shining examples of people born in difficult circumstances who've gone on to lead exemplary lives – and we've also seen the opposite, where rich, spoilt children go astray. But without exactly experiencing someone else's life we simply can't make any judgment. We *can* proudly proclaim: '*I* would *never* allow myself to behave like that!' – and we can *hope* that's true. But, because we've never actually faced the totality of that person's experience, we just can't be so sure.

This in turn leads us onto the question that has baffled and perplexed ever since we invented the idea of a single, supreme deity: how can one individual be born with all the advantages of a family where there's plenty of money and love to go round, while another suffers abject poverty and all the worst excesses of degradation and lack – of love, money, everything?

At some point most of us allow ourselves to wonder what kind of supreme being allows that degree of unfairness, just as we ask how wonderful people who don't seem to deserve it can die young – even as children who had their whole lives ahead of them? When the only answer monotheistic religions can offer is that 'God moves in mysterious ways', it can be enough to drive us away completely.

Many people have turned to other ways of looking at this, in particular to the idea of reincarnation. The argument is that if we have many lives we get to experience all the different extremes, and everything ends up fair for all. Some people have gone as far as to claim that Jesus himself preached the concept of reincarnation, but that it was deliberately omitted from the scriptures – because it didn't fit with a doctrine where the choice was between behaving oneself to gain salvation or misbehaving and suffering eternal damnation.

To many people this probably sounds interesting and persuasive. But it's actually unlikely – the reason being that our traditional concepts of reincarnation are almost certainly way too simplistic.

The modern OOB and other evidence does suggest that our true soul consciousness has many life experiences, in this reality and many others too. But, as hard as it is for us to grasp, it also strongly suggests that they're all happening *at the same time*.[1] So that

---

[1] I discuss the evidence for this idea at length in my books *Supersoul* and *The Power of You*, along with the various new concepts I've developed to make sense of it – such as that of the 'supersoul', of 'birth givens' and of 'resonant souls'. Again these books contain copious quotations and source references.

aspect of us that's acting out the part of a medieval knight, an Egyptian princess, a caveman or whatever is somehow operating *alongside* us. Even though it's so hard for us to imagine, their life is still ongoing.

What this also means is there can be no such thing as karma being carried from one life to the next. It simply can't work in such a simplistic way if all lives are simultaneous. It makes much more sense that each actor in each play is responsible for their *own* experience, and for what they create in that experience as they go along via their thoughts, intentions, beliefs and so on. Put another way, it would completely violate our free will to create our experience in whatever way we choose if some other actor in some other apparent timeframe was having a major impact on us.

WHAT JESUS WAS REALLY SAYING

Faced with all this, how else can we answer the question about the apparent inequalities between different people's lives? One thing is clear, we are each born with a set of what we might call 'birth givens' that have a huge impact on our subsequent lives.

So who decides what these are – our sex, our main psychological, emotional and physical traits, the characters of our parents and other family members, their socio-economic position and geographic location, and so on? Is it God? No, because he, she or it doesn't exist in any conventional sense. What we're left with is that it must be our true soul consciousness itself – which tries out myriads of different combinations of birth givens, and then gives each of its creations the free will to make what they will of their lot:

Each of us has to paint the best picture

> But why does the soul consciousness follow this course?

we can using the palette we've been given by the higher, divine aspect of ourselves.

That is our purpose in life. Nothing more, nothing less. It is as simple as that.

We might refer to this true, divine soul consciousness that encompasses many lives at once as our *super*soul, to distinguish it from the merely soul consciousness that we retain after death. All the OOB and other evidence suggests that this latter continues to have all sorts of experiences in the higher realms but – and this is the crucial part – it tends to continue to identify with the actor of the play just experienced. None of the most reliable evidence suggests that it prepares itself to return for another incarnation.

So how does our supersoul relate to our concept of God? The answer is that as a human being the former is as close as we'll ever get to understanding what true divinity is, and it's why we can reasonably make the claim that each of us is a god in our own right. Supersouls are the very entities who create whole new universes that operate under totally different rules when they feel like changing and expanding the game. But each supersoul is still very much an individual entity and, to provide some context, it seems likely that myriads of supersouls are involved just in this game we call 'life on planet earth'.

Our supersoul, then, is far, far removed from any concept of a 'universal consciousness' – which is what most of us mean when we refer to God. But it also seems likely that anyone who thinks they've made even fleeting contact with the 'All', the 'One' or 'Source' – or whatever they want to call that incredible sense of oneness, stillness and peace that some are fortunate enough to experience via deep meditation or other altered states – is simply mistaken. Rather it would seem likely that that's what contact with your own *supersoul* feels like.

This also means that any speculation about what's going on at any substantially higher or more refined levels is likely to be futile. It seems that even our broadest possible concept of *our* universe and *our* reality is just the tiniest speck in the totality of all the possible and probable universes and realities that exist at different levels of vibration and frequency.

It can be useful to think of these as endless computer-style simulations being played out by different levels of consciousness. As long as it doesn't conjure up images of humanity being slaves to whoever's in control of the game – which is absolutely *not* what's being described here.

None of the foregoing means we should airily dismiss the countless millions of people who over the last two thousand years have gained huge strength and comfort from believing that Jesus or God is looking after them. Or the countless people who've led good, honest, loving lives, and even laid them down, in Jesus' name. Or the countless people who've been devoted to helping others less fortunate than themselves. Nobody can reasonably dismiss all that as misguided.

But nor can we reasonably ignore the terrible damage organised religion has wrought, and continues to wreak, in countless conflicts around the globe; or the shocking sex scandals involving priests; and so on and so forth. Leading atheists and materialists concentrate on these issues to such an extent that they write the whole thing off, and also tend to scoff at the supposed stupidity of those who have faith and belief. But of course that's not the answer either.

We should be in no doubt that it's far more intelligent and logical to form our view of the world based on the multitude of modern evidence that our experience is not just a 'physical' one, than it is to adopt the materialist view that the brain is the source of consciousness and that everything ends at death.

We should also be in no doubt that we're fundamentally spiritual beings having a human experience, rather than human beings who might or might not believe in anything spiritual.

But – and it's a massive but – there's a whole world of difference between the controlling nature of organised religion and the liberation and empowerment of true spirituality.

WHAT JESUS WAS REALLY SAYING

In much of the Western world support for orthodox Christianity is fading fast. In many communities church congregations are falling and young people aren't being attracted in. It is highly likely that the major reason for this is that the words in the hymns sung and in the passages of scripture read out simply don't *resonate* with a modern generation brought up to question things.

If one revisits the four gospels, for example, one is struck by the sheer inconsistency and downright incomprehensibility of much of what Jesus is supposed to have said. What is more the knots that Christian commentators tie themselves up in trying to make them make sense render the whole ensemble even less reasonable and credible. It seems that in a modern, rational world we have little option but to face the fact that what purports to be holy and sacred scripture

Write a hymn, Ian!

← *meant in a good way.*

is nothing of the sort.

At which point we can either abandon the whole lot. Or we can look for those all-important kernels of truth that lie hidden underneath all the distortions.

they weren't miracles

WHAT JESUS WAS REALLY SAYING

Any attempt to restore Jesus' true messages for humanity is potentially problematic in that, as we've already seen, the four gospels contain serious differences in terms of the key events. In this chapter we're primarily interested in his more celebrated miracles, and there are clear discrepancies in the reporting of their order or their details in different gospels. Despite this, the fact that multiple major miracles are scattered throughout the four accounts means we can perhaps allow ourselves to assume, with reasonable justification, that *something* out of the ordinary was being reported. The same can also be said of his healing activities discussed in the next chapter.

That having been said, in the remainder of this book we'll be indulging in a considerable amount of speculation concerning the interpretation of selected passages in the gospels. It is all we can

WHAT JESUS WAS REALLY SAYING

do when attempting to work from records that have been so badly distorted. There can be no question that not all of this speculation, especially perhaps in the later chapters, will be correct.

That doesn't, however, detract from the evidence in support of our *fundamental* premise – which is that Jesus was trying to show us that any of us has the ability to manipulate this reality we're experiencing, potentially in quite extreme ways.

To begin at the beginning:

Then Jesus was led up by the Spirit into the wilderness to be tempted by the devil. He fasted for forty days and forty nights. (Matthew 4:1-2)

Most accounts seem to suggest that Jesus' real work only started when he came back from this sojourn 'in the wilderness'. In the Jewish culture of the time the expression 'forty days and nights' was not specific, but simply meant 'a long time'. That aside, if this aspect of his story is at all reliable then what was he really doing there? After all we know he wasn't really being tempted by the devil because we've seen that there's no such entity. But what if he was testing *himself*?

It is commonly understood that tribal culture always involves some sort of initiation process for adolescent males to make the transition into adulthood, which often involves being sent out into the wild with no food. This is designed, at least in part, to bring on altered states of consciousness.

Learning to control and manipulate our 'physical' reality in the way Jesus did is a serious challenge, and would almost certainly require some sort of focused practice. It makes sense that he would want to do this away from prying eyes and with full concentration.

Jesus was preparing himself for some serious acts of manipulation, as we'll shortly see. But we shouldn't lose sight of the fact that many people share similar but more easily mastered gifts that defy normal materialist explanation – such as telepathy, precognition, telekinesis, spiritual healing and so on.

Just like any others, these skills are developed to different degrees in each of us as part of our birth givens. Jesus' latent ability to manipulate reality – or, more likely, his *built-in understanding* and *unshakeable belief* that he was able to do it – was almost certainly particularly accentuated, but not to the extent that he was fundamentally different from any of us. It is the very fact that ultimately he was here entirely in human form that gives his messages, and even more his practical demonstrations of his skills, so much relevance and power. But also, precisely because he was only human, he had to put work in to master them.

It is likely that he and those close to him would've realised he wasn't just an ordinary boy from a relatively early age. But even then, if he had a strong sense of his destiny and of what he'd need to achieve as an adult, he would've wanted to make sure his secret stayed at home. In the intolerant climate of the time, any premature revelation would almost certainly have foiled that destiny.

It is not impossible that, by the time he went out into the wilderness, he would perhaps have been ready to deliberately foster altered states of consciousness by limiting his intake of food, and that combined with complete isolation would've allowed him to hone the harder-to-master skills until he was ready to start using them in public.

Once he was ready to make his mark, where to begin? We can't know for sure because of the uncertainty about the order of events, but according to John he started in the everyday environment of a party, in front of plenty of observers:

On the third day there was a wedding in Cana of Galilee… When the wine gave out, the mother of Jesus said to him, 'They have no wine…' His mother said to the servants, 'Do whatever he tells you…' Jesus said to them, 'Fill the jars with water.' And they filled them up to the brim… When the steward tasted the water that had become wine, [he] did not know where it came from (though the servants who had drawn the water knew)... Jesus did this, the first of his signs, in Cana of Galilee, and revealed his glory; and his disciples believed in him. (John 2:1-11)

There is a certain groundedness to the speculation that this was the event that really got the ball rolling. After all, who wouldn't want to know someone who could produce wine out of nowhere?

In any case a similarly startling event on an even larger scale occurred with the celebrated loaves and fish:

When it was evening, the disciples came to him and said, 'This is a deserted place, and the hour is now late; send the crowds away so that they may go into the villages and buy food for themselves.' Jesus said to them, 'They need not go away; you give them something to eat.' They replied, 'We have nothing here

WHAT JESUS WAS REALLY SAYING

but five loaves and two fish.' And he said, 'Bring them here to me.' Then he ordered the crowds to sit down on the grass. Taking the five loaves and the two fish, he looked up to heaven, and blessed and broke the loaves, and gave them to the disciples, and the disciples gave them to the crowds. And all ate and were filled; and they took up what was left over of the broken pieces, twelve baskets full. And those who ate were about five thousand men, besides women and children. (Matthew 14:14-21)

For many people these stories of supposed miracles probably evoke distant memories of Bible study as a child – and a recognition that many of us then tended to grow somewhat cynical as, in time, we started to question many aspects of Christian religious doctrine. But perhaps now we can see there may

WHAT JESUS WAS REALLY SAYING

be some substance to these accounts after all. It's just they require a completely different interpretation from the traditional one.

Our contention is that they weren't miracles at all. Instead Jesus was manipulating the shared experience of physical reality in the same way we all do all the time. The only difference is that most of the time we're doing it purely subconsciously, not actively directing what we experience – and that most of us aren't yet ready to believe we can convert water into wine or create unlimited food from only a few loaves and fishes. But if we think back to the sportsperson raising themselves above all their highly skilled competitors, or the mother desperate to save her child – both succeeding in their endeavours by sheer force of will and imagination alone – it's not too much of a stretch to recognise that what Jesus was doing was only an extension of that.

There were many other examples of miracles, but some were only witnessed by his closest followers. It seems likely that he particularly wanted to teach them what he was doing because he knew they'd have to carry on with his mission of education once he was gone:

He said to Simon, 'Put out into the deep water and let down your nets for a catch.' Simon answered, 'Master, we have worked all night long but have caught nothing. Yet if you say so, I will let down the nets.' When they had done this, they caught so many fish that their nets were beginning to break. So they signalled to their partners in the other boat to come and help them. And they came and filled both boats, so that they began to sink. (Luke 5:3-7)

WHAT JESUS WAS REALLY SAYING

It seems he also wanted to teach them that they could even control the forces of nature, if they really put their minds to it:

> *A gale arose on the lake, so great that the boat was being swamped by the waves; but he was asleep. And they went and woke him up, saying, 'Lord, save us! We are perishing!' And he said to them, 'Why are you afraid, you of little faith?' Then he got up and rebuked the winds and the sea; and there was a dead calm. They were amazed, saying, 'What sort of man is this, that even the winds and the sea obey him?' (Matthew 8:23-27)*

What is more there are a few surviving examples of him deliberately challenging them to copy what he was doing, so that they learned the practice as well as the theory:

WHAT JESUS WAS REALLY SAYING

Early in the morning he came walking towards them on the lake. But when the disciples saw him walking on the lake, they were terrified, saying, 'It is a ghost!' And they cried out in fear. But immediately Jesus spoke to them and said, 'Take heart, it is I; do not be afraid.' Peter answered him, 'Lord, if it is you, command me to come to you on the water.' He said, 'Come.' So Peter got out of the boat, started walking on the water, and came towards Jesus. But when he noticed the strong wind, he became frightened, and beginning to sink, he cried out, 'Lord, save me!' Jesus immediately reached out his hand and caught him, saying to him, 'You of little faith, why did you doubt?' (Matthew 14:23-31)

Now the disciples had forgotten to bring any bread; and they had only one loaf with them in the boat... And becoming aware of it, Jesus said to them, 'Why are you talking about having no bread? Do you still not perceive or understand? Are your hearts hardened? Do you have eyes, and fail to see? Do you have ears, and fail to hear? And do you not remember? When I broke the five loaves for the five thousand, how many baskets full of broken pieces did you collect?' They said to him, 'Twelve.' 'And the seven for the four thousand, how many baskets full of broken pieces did you collect?' And they said to him, 'Seven.' Then he said to them, 'Do you not yet understand?' (Mark 8:14-21)

In the last three passages Jesus is reported as having rebuked his followers for their lack of faith. It seems highly likely that this aspect has been massively exaggerated in our versions of the gospels to widen the perceived gap between him and them – making him look ever more divine and them more human. But if he was only human it's also possible that he may at times have become a little frustrated by their lack of belief in their own abilities.

On rare occasions it seems he may have really pushed the boundaries – one example being when he transformed himself so that his true 'energy body' shone before them:

Six days later, Jesus took with him Peter and James and his brother John and led them up a high mountain, by themselves. And he was transfigured before them, and his face shone like the sun, and his clothes became dazzling white. (Matthew 17:1)

His ultimate demonstration, though, was that death itself is merely a mirage:

Mary Magdalene and the other Mary went to see the tomb. And suddenly there was a great earthquake; for an angel of the Lord, descending from heaven, came and rolled back the stone and sat on it. His appearance was like lightning, and his clothing white as snow. For fear of him the guards shook and became like dead men. But the angel said to the women, 'Do not be afraid; I know that you are looking for Jesus who was crucified. He is not here; for he has been raised, as he said. Come, see the place where he lay. Then go quickly and tell his disciples, "He has been raised from the dead, and indeed he is going ahead of you to Galilee; there you will see him." This is my message for you.' So they left the tomb quickly with fear and great joy, and ran to tell his disciples. Suddenly Jesus met them and said, 'Greetings!' And they came to him, took hold of his feet, and worshipped him. Then Jesus said to them, 'Do not be afraid; go and tell my brothers to go to Galilee; there they will see me.' (Matthew 28:1-10)

Some of the worst distortions in the gospels almost certainly surround accounts like this of what happened immediately after his death. If there's any substance to them at all, let's consider if any more reasonable explanations exist. First of all, if his tomb was found empty it would almost certainly be because it was *robbed* – just as there's plenty of evidence that those of the pharaohs of Egypt were plundered only shortly after their internment, which explains their ever more ingenious attempts at security to prevent their bodies and riches from being stolen. If all Jesus had was a large stone, rolled into place by Roman soldiers with long levers, it seems equally likely that some enterprising individuals felt that by reversing the process and stealing his body they might make some useful money from his mortal remains.

What about the idea of a resurrection – of him somehow cheating death and coming back in his original physical body? Such an account may have suited those who wanted to make the story more elaborate and miraculous, allowing the Church fathers to then weave onto it the idea that he died and rose again to atone for everyone else's sins. But again this is almost certainly just another idea that was dreamed up to manipulate the masses.

Why? First, we've already seen that

there's no such thing as evil, so nor can there be any such thing as inherent sin. Second, no one – not even Jesus – can take away our own responsibility for our own behaviour.

As to what might really have happened if there's any substance to these resurrection accounts, let's cast our minds back to the fact that many departed souls become trapped in the earth plane after death, and that people with finely tuned perception can see them as ghosts. If Jesus had mastered the manipulation of the physical plane while incarnated in it, how much easier would it have been for him to master being a ghost?

Except if the reports are true he took it to the extent of lowering his vibrations sufficiently that his followers could actually reach out and touch him. This is something most departed souls find too difficult to achieve, even though they would love to be able to touch their loved ones. But let's not forget it's commonly reported that the intense emotional energy of more disturbed poltergeists allows them to fling objects around, which is a step along the path of being able to manipulate the physical from the ethereal. So this too doesn't need to be interpreted as miraculous. It was simply another example of Jesus manipulating energies – this time from a different reality.

faith can move

mountains

WHAT JESUS WAS REALLY SAYING

'For truly I tell you, if you have faith the size of a mustard seed, you will say to this mountain, "Move from here to there", and it will move; and nothing will be impossible for you.'
(Matthew 17:20-21)

Nowhere has Jesus' fundamental message been better preserved than in this short passage. It tells us absolutely that we have unlimited power to shape the illusion we're currently experiencing. Of course most of us won't get anywhere near moving mountains in the literal sense – after all, why would we want to? But he was deliberately using it as an extreme example.

The word used in this passage is *faith*, which has of course been taken to mean faith in Jesus, or in God. But in this next passage a better context emerges:

'Truly I tell you, if you say to this mountain, "Be taken up and thrown

into the sea", and if you do not doubt in your heart, but believe that what you say will come to pass, it will be done for you. So I tell you, whatever you ask for in prayer, believe that you have received it, and it will be yours.' (Mark 11:23-24)

It is a subtle difference, but the use of the word *belief* here better makes the point that, in order to shape our reality as we prefer it, we don't need faith in someone else – like Jesus or God, for example. Instead we simply need to understand and *believe* in the fundamental workings of our reality. The simple fact is that anything we *fully* believe in our heart and *fully* focus on with our mind will come true – or, more accurately, will manifest in our 'physical' experience. It cannot help but do so. Unless we don't really believe in what we're doing and give out conflicting directions to the underlying mechanisms of the universe – often at a less conscious level – as we'll see in the next chapter.

The other word used in this passage is *prayer*, and to some extent it doesn't really matter whether we think we're praying to God or creating the desired outcome for ourselves. What matters is the extent to which we believe in the outcome – although in a broader sense it's far better if we take responsibility for our own creations.

Considering all the distortions of editing and translation, it's remarkable that another crucial sentiment seems to have been preserved in the phrase 'believe that you have received it'. Those who express their belief to the maximum act as if they've *already achieved* the outcome they desire. This idea has been expressed in many of the contemporary books on the subject of manifestation, reality creation, the law of attraction and so on.

The most commonly recorded of Jesus' supposed miracles were the healings he performed everywhere he went – although we can safely ignore the contemporary attribution of many illnesses to possession by demons:

> *Jesus went throughout Galilee, teaching in their synagogues and proclaiming the good news of the kingdom and curing every disease and every sickness among the people. So his fame spread throughout all Syria, and they brought to him all the sick, those who were afflicted with various diseases and pains, demoniacs, epileptics, and paralytics, and he cured them. (Matthew 4:23-24)*

Aside from the charlatans that any aspect of human society inevitably attracts, since time immemorial there have been spiritual healers spread around the world who can do what Jesus did. But the crucial and often-overlooked factor is that, like him, they're powerless to heal someone else unless that person actively seeks them out *and* fully believes in their potential to be healed. That's how free will and the law of attraction continue to operate even in this area. Indeed often the patient is effectively healing *themselves*, merely using the healer as a catalyst to focus their belief.

The reports of his healing work with individuals reveal just how important was the afflicted person's belief that they'd be cured:

> *Then suddenly a woman who had been suffering from haemorrhages*

WHAT JESUS WAS REALLY SAYING

for twelve years came up behind him and touched the fringe of his cloak, for she said to herself, 'If I only touch his cloak, I will be made well.' Jesus turned, and seeing her he said, 'Take heart, daughter; your faith has made you well.' And instantly the woman was made well. (Matthew 9:20-22)

As he and his disciples and a large crowd were leaving Jericho, Bartimaeus son of Timaeus, a blind beggar, was sitting by the roadside. When he heard that it was Jesus of Nazareth, he began to shout out and say, 'Jesus, Son of David, have mercy on me!' Many sternly ordered him to be quiet, but he cried out even more loudly, 'Son of David, have mercy on me!' Jesus stood still and said, 'Call him here.' And they called the blind man, saying to him, 'Take heart; get up,

WHAT JESUS WAS REALLY SAYING

he is calling you.' So throwing off his cloak, he sprang up and came to Jesus. Then Jesus said to him, 'What do you want me to do for you?' The blind man said to him, 'My teacher, let me see again.' Jesus said to him, 'Go; your faith has made you well.' Immediately he regained his sight and followed him on the way. (Mark 10:46-52)

When he had come down from the mountain, great crowds followed him; and there was a leper who came to him and knelt before him, saying, 'Lord, if you choose, you can make me clean.' He stretched out his hand and touched him, saying, 'I do choose. Be made clean!' Immediately his leprosy was cleansed. (Matthew 8:1-3)

When he entered the house, the blind men came to him; and Jesus said to them, 'Do you believe that I am able to do this?' They said to him, 'Yes, Lord.' Then he touched their eyes and said, 'According to your faith let it be done to you.' And their eyes were opened. (Matthew 9:28-30)

Having said that, in the next three reports the belief of those *close to* the afflicted person was the dominant factor. Indeed in these cases their love seems to have overcome all. But we might surmise that, even if only at a subconscious level, the afflicted people themselves also had the requisite belief and desire:

When he returned to Capernaum after some days, it was reported that he was at home. So many gathered around that there was no longer room for them, not even in front of the door; and he was

WHAT JESUS WAS REALLY SAYING

speaking the word to them. Then some people came, bringing to him a paralysed man, carried by four of them. And when they could not bring him to Jesus because of the crowd, they removed the roof above him; and after having dug through it, they let down the mat on which the paralytic lay. When Jesus saw their faith, he said to the paralytic, 'Son, your sins are forgiven... I say to you, stand up, take your mat and go to your home.' And he stood up, and immediately took the mat and went out before all of them. (Mark 2:1-12)

When he entered Capernaum, a centurion came to him, appealing to him and saying, 'Lord, my servant is lying at home paralysed, in terrible distress.' And he said to him, 'I will come and cure him.' The

WHAT JESUS WAS REALLY SAYING

centurion answered, 'Lord, I am not worthy to have you come under my roof; but only speak the word, and my servant will be healed. For I also am a man under authority, with soldiers under me; and I say to one, "Go", and he goes, and to another, "Come", and he comes, and to my slave, "Do this", and the slave does it.' When Jesus heard him, he was amazed and said to those who followed him, 'Truly I tell you, in no one in Israel have I found such faith... And to the centurion Jesus said, 'Go; let it be done for you according to your faith.' And the servant was healed in that hour. (Matthew 8:5-13)

Jesus left that place and went away to the district of Tyre and Sidon. Just then a Canaanite woman from that region came out and started shouting, 'Have mercy on me, Lord,

WHAT JESUS WAS REALLY SAYING

Son of David; my daughter is tormented by a demon'... Then Jesus answered her, 'Woman, great is your faith! Let it be done for you as you wish.' And her daughter was healed instantly. (Matthew 15:21-28)

It is worth noting that in the last two reports he didn't even need to be in the presence of the afflicted person. This is what we now refer to as *distance* or *remote* healing, and there are many who practice this too in the modern world.

The importance of faith or belief is emphasised in the passages we quoted in the previous chapter about purported miracles. Although they almost certainly tend to exaggerate the extent to which Jesus rebuked his followers, the key issue was their *lack* of faith in being able to effect what were admittedly quite major manipulations of reality – such as calming a storm, walking on water or replicating food.

But he's also reported as having done this on lesser occasions involving, for example, healing – although his supposedly angry and arrogant attitude is probably even more exaggerated here:

> When they came to the crowd, a man came to him, knelt before him, and said, 'Lord, have mercy on my son, for he is an epileptic and he suffers terribly; he often falls into the fire and often into the water. And I brought him to your disciples, but they could not cure him.' Jesus answered, 'You faithless and perverse generation, how much longer must I be with you? How much longer must I put up with you? Bring him here to me.' And Jesus rebuked the demon, and it came out of him, and the boy was

typical Middle East.

cured instantly. Then the disciples came to Jesus privately and said, 'Why could we not cast it out?' He said to them, 'Because of your little faith.' (Matthew 17:14-20)

The same lack of faith and belief was evident when he returned to his home town. We might surmise that as a group they saw him grow up as a relatively ordinary child, and so knew him too well to believe what he was showing them when he returned – to the point that he couldn't work effectively there:

He came to his home town and began to teach the people in their synagogue, so that they were astounded and said, 'Where did this man get this wisdom and these deeds of power? Is not this the carpenter's son? Is not his mother called Mary? And are not his brothers James and Joseph and

Simon and Judas? And are not all his sisters with us? Where then did this man get all this?' And they took offence at him. But Jesus said to them, 'Prophets are not without honour except in their own country and in their own house.' And he did not do many deeds of power there, because of their unbelief. (Matthew 13:54-58)

The final test of faith and belief for his followers arose when he was apparently resurrected – and in this version he again berates them for their lack of it:

Now after he rose early on the first day of the week, he appeared first to Mary Magdalene... She went out and told those who had been with him, while they were mourning and weeping. But when they heard that he was alive and had been seen by her, they would not believe it. After

WHAT JESUS WAS REALLY SAYING

this he appeared in another form to two of them, as they were walking into the country. And they went back and told the rest, but they did not believe them. Later he appeared to the eleven themselves as they were sitting at the table; and he upbraided them for their lack of faith and stubbornness, because they had not believed those who saw him after he had risen. (Mark 16:9-14)

It might appear that Jesus' more extreme manipulations of reality — such as walking on water, turning it into wine, replicating food and controlling the weather — have little to do with our everyday lives. We might even be tempted to say the same of spiritual healing, although our attitude might change if we ever found ourselves attracting serious illness.

WHAT JESUS WAS REALLY SAYING

What is most important, of course, is for each of us to take control of our own, everyday experience. But it's worth emphasising that, according to all the ethereal or channelled sources who support the idea that we're each responsible for creating our own reality, there's no real difference between these things. In other words that *theoretically* moving a mountain is just as easy as attracting a new partner or more money or whatever we most desire. They all involve manipulating a reality that sees no difference between these outcomes — other than the difference in our own level of belief in relation to them.

So let's be absolutely clear that there's actually no such thing as easy or hard manipulations, except in our perception. If we want we can reach for the stars straight away. Alternatively, at least at the outset, most of us will be content just to learn to control our everyday reality on a more basic level. Let us be clear that *both* these paths are equally valid expressions of our divinity.

*there are
no victims*

WHAT JESUS WAS REALLY SAYING

'Enter through the narrow gate; for the gate is wide and the road is easy that leads to destruction, and there are many who take it. For the gate is narrow and the road is hard that leads to life, and there are few who find it.' (Matthew 7:13-14)

This is an enigmatic passage, and the interpretation that follows is undoubtedly speculative. But it just might hold an important clue to how we can escape from the addiction to suffering noted in the second chapter.

Some especially eastern cultures fully recognise this addiction and attempt to teach people how to avoid it. But unfortunately their worldview is somewhat at variance with the one outlined in the early chapters – as is their advice about how to live.

That is because they understand that life's an illusion but, rather like the

WHAT JESUS WAS REALLY SAYING

Gnostics who were Jesus' contemporaries, they tend to see the physical world as something of an abomination – from which we should be trying to escape. What is more, when this is allied to a relatively traditional view of reincarnation into successive lives, the supposed recipe can be to virtually withdraw from active life to escape from the 'wheel of karma'.

But surely this is simply another illusion. We have already seen that our world can be thought of as a game that our divine supersoul consciousness has helped to create and wants to explore. What it *really* wants is for us to recognise it's an illusion that can be manipulated so that we can enjoy it as much as possible – because our world is absolutely *not* an abomination. But our supersoul also knows that the illusion is so persuasive that remembering what's really going on, and why we're here, is seriously difficult.

So what can we do about our addiction to suffering? The first thing to understand is that it manifests itself as a marked tendency towards being a victim. What is more we can be a victim in many ways. As we saw earlier, when things don't work out how we hoped we blame God, or our past lives and our karma, or our life plan, or blind chance. More prosaically when undesirable events happen we nearly always manage to make it the fault of our partner, our parents, our siblings, our boss, our colleagues or our friends. All of these are ways to avoid taking responsibility for what we *ourselves* are creating.

As phlegmatic as we might think it sounds, even taking the popular view that 'it's just not meant to be' is a mild from of victimhood. Instead there's *only* what we do or don't *attract*.

WHAT JESUS WAS REALLY SAYING

It may be because seeing through the illusion and deciding to take control of our own life is such a big step that Jesus originally told us 'the gate is narrow and the road is hard'. But it's the only path that leads to *life* – that is a life of joyful abundance, minus all the suffering.

What follows needs to be thought about carefully, because it's the real key to mastering the illusion:

In order to create the life we want, we need to understand that we're already creating the life we're having – all of it, all the time, in every moment, with no exceptions. So none of us is a victim, ever, of anyone or anything. We're always in the driving seat.

We are creating the entirety of our experience – as explained earlier, not just via our proactive thoughts and intentions, but also via our underlying beliefs, preconceptions and attitudes.

These are strong statements that will be extremely hard for some people to accept – especially if, for example, they or a loved one has contracted a serous illness, or someone close to them has died before their time. Such a person will understandably look at their life, or that of their loved one, and insist there's no way they could've *attracted* that.

The key issue here is that there are certain mitigations. Children for example aren't fully responsible for their lives until they grow up and achieve independence. So any major challenges they face will tend to form part of their birth givens, rather than being something they've attracted.

In addition it seems that our divine supersoul consciousness *might* occasionally present us with additional challenges as an adult – perhaps because they feel we can handle them as an additional part of our experience, perhaps even because we've done better than expected in learning how to cope with any challenges we've already faced related, for example, to our birth givens. This would mean these new challenges weren't something we'd attracted, at least not in the conventional sense. But we should aim to regard such *un*attracted challenges as a rare occurrence – certainly to the extent they apply to ourselves – otherwise we can tend to lapse into victimhood again.

All this has some very important implications for how we lead our life:

We may not always be able to understand exactly how we attracted certain major challenges into our life but, if we err on the side of caution and assume we must have done so, we make sure we take full responsibility –

especially for our reaction to them.

We talked earlier about not living in the apparent past, and we might see this as just another moment when that can be applied. Some people suddenly hit by a major challenge might decide there's no point worrying about *why* it happened – all that matters is accepting that it is what it is, and making the decision that they can control how they *react* to it.

On the other hand some people might want to look at the dynamics of how they might have attracted said challenge so they can learn not to attract it again, even if they only do this some time later when the dust has settled.

Either of these is a perfectly valid way of handling it. What we *don't* want to do is drift into victim mode.

Perhaps this is what Jesus was really trying to tell us in the following parable:

WHAT JESUS WAS REALLY SAYING

'Why do you call me "Lord, Lord", and do not do what I tell you? I will show you what someone is like who comes to me, hears my words, and acts on them. That one is like a man building a house, who dug deeply and laid the foundation on rock; when a flood arose, the river burst against that house but could not shake it, because it had been well built. But the one who hears and does not act is like a man who built a house on the ground without a foundation. When the river burst against it, immediately it fell, and great was the ruin of that house.'
(Luke 6:46-49)

Do we want to be someone who's happy to take responsibility for our creations in the good times, but then blames someone or something else in the bad times? Or do we want to be steady and strong and take responsibility for the *entirety* of our experience?

All this puts us in a position to come to certain further strong conclusions:

Victimhood is suffering. It places us in a position where we feel we're not in control, and at the mercy of someone or something else. That always leads to stress and hurt. By contrast it's very hard to suffer when we feel we are in control. It naturally follows that if we take full responsibility for everything we experience in our life, our suffering will vanish. So taking responsibility isn't a burden to be avoided – it's the ultimate in self empowerment.

We might come to understand, then, that however unhappy our life may be we *can* change it. We may have to take small steps at first but there's no situation that can't be improved. In actuality anyone's life can be transformed *in an instant* if they have sufficient belief, but for most of us the transition will take a little time and patience. Yet all the evidence suggests we *can* change it for the better, if we *choose*.

Jesus told us all those centuries ago that if we followed his example it would free us from suffering. Although the following passages have been interpreted in a completely different way, maybe he was really advising us to simply copy the way he took responsibility:

> *'Come to me, all you that are weary and are carrying heavy burdens, and I will give you rest. Take my yoke upon you, and learn from me; for I am gentle and humble in heart, and you will find rest for your souls.' (Matthew 11:28-30)*
>
> *'The Spirit of the Lord is upon me, because he has anointed me to*

bring good news to the poor. He has sent me to proclaim release to the captives and recovery of sight to the blind, to let the oppressed go free.' (Luke 4:16-18)

He almost certainly didn't mean those who were literally blind, but those who suffer because they don't understand the illusions of our reality.

So how do we make the change? The key skill is to become aware of and control what are often called our *limiting* thoughts and beliefs. In other words if we believe we're unworthy of love, friendship, success or whatever, we'll continue to create a reality in which these things elude us.

Often these beliefs have been instilled in us since childhood, and they can be hard to spot because they're so ingrained in our subconscious. Perhaps the following passage was meant to convey the idea that we need to learn to interpret the underlying patterns that are conditioning our life experience – in just the same way that we interpret more obvious ones:

> *'When you see a cloud rising in the west, you immediately say, "It is going to rain"; and so it happens. And when you see the south wind blowing, you say, "There will be scorching heat"; and it happens... You know how to interpret the appearance of earth and sky, but why do you not know how to interpret the present time?' (Luke 12:54-56)*

So, if we're unhappy with any part of our life, we might ask ourselves: 'what underlying belief must I hold to be creating this?' Once we've unearthed it, then we can start to change it.

The associated skill we'll need to develop

to help with all this is to train our 'observer self' to watch out for limiting beliefs arising in our thoughts, to catch them before they can take hold, and to replace them with more desirable ones.

Some people *might* be able to make these changes alone and immediately, because for them change is actually a *decision* rather than a process. For example the decision to no longer be a victim, *ever*, is one of the most liberating and powerful we can make.

But others may need more time. There are plenty of books available to help with all this, and in more severe cases various forms of therapy are available – although we should always be wary of trying to offload responsibility, because ultimately it's *us* who has to want to change, and *us* who has to make it happen.

The other thing to be aware of is that many of our limiting beliefs are culturally impressed. Our modern world is actually far more fear-ridden than in the past. We have insurance companies and medical professionals constantly firing every possible bad scenario at us – the risk of serious illness, or of being robbed, or of our home burning down – and, guess what? If we give these things our attention we run a high risk of attracting them into our life. But there *is* an alternative. We can take ourselves out of the mainstream, dare to be different and simply make the decision: 'I *will not* give these things my attention.'

What is more in the modern world it's pretty widely recognised that nearly all illness originates in the mind – at least in adults. That's not to say we're all hypochondriacs, but all mental stresses and strains have to find an outlet in the end, and usually it's in some sort of bodily malady. Eliminating stress and worry from our life as much as possible is an absolute necessity if we want to stay healthy long-term.

Of course some people believe *their* life is just way too busy and complicated for this – but if so they would do well to remember that stress doesn't arise from being *busy* but from feeling we're *not in control*. So we need to take the control back, in whatever way works for us.

Having said that single parents, for example, or those caring for an elderly relative or partner, face a hugely trying job day in, day out – yet most of them do it with huge love and selflessness. But we shouldn't forget that there's little difference between martyrdom and victimhood, and both should be avoided at all costs. Helping others with joy, not as a duty or out of guilt, is the only way to truly express love for them.

So whatever challenges we're facing, we *can* make changes to our lifestyle – and even more to our *perception* of our life – that will improve it and give us a degree of control back, if we so *choose*.

Finally we should remember Jesus' advice about asking for help:

'So I say to you, ask, and it will be given to you; search, and you will find; knock, and the door will be opened for you. For everyone who asks receives, and everyone who searches finds, and for everyone who knocks, the door will be opened.' (Luke 11:9-10)

In terms of our new worldview, although our divine supersoul consciousness won't tend to interfere in our life *unbidden* – because it wants us to take responsibility and work things out for ourselves – it will always *respond* in some way to a request for help if we feel we need it. It just may not be in the most obvious way that we might expect.

*the past is
the past*

WHAT JESUS WAS REALLY SAYING

'No one who puts a hand to the plough and looks back is fit for the kingdom of God.' (Luke 9:62)

This is one of *the* most important of all Jesus' preserved pronouncements. We saw in the third chapter that, as hard as it is for our human mind to grasp, all the personalities projected by our divine supersoul consciousness are in actuality living *alongside* each other – irrespective of the human era in which they appear to be operating.

This is because what we call 'time' is not an endless continuum as we perceive it, but in fact a discrete series of 'now moments'. Many spiritual teachers both ancient and modern have emphasised that 'everything is happening in the now' because 'now is all that exists'. But we often fail to understand the practical implications for our everyday life.

This isn't a major surprise, because our

entire human conditioning is to use associations from what we perceive as 'past' events to determine how we'll act in any given now moment. It was fundamental to our survival as a species in the early years, and still is now to some extent. For example, we all learn early on that if we put our hand into a flame it hurts, and so on.

The trouble is we carry this over into all areas of our life, and often use past associations to bolster our sense of victimhood. How often do we hear people say, 'I always attract the wrong sort of partner', or 'if there's bad luck going it will find me', or 'I'm always broke and I never have enough money'?

Of course some people's negativity is much worse than others, but even those who mainly adopt a positive outlook will have one or two areas of their lives where past association is with failure. So our observer self should always be on the lookout for any statements like this we might make.

The truth is that life doesn't *have* to be like that. Each new situation that comes along doesn't *have* to follow the same script as before. We *can* change it, simply by refusing to let past associations play a part. Again it'll fall to our observer self to notice when we're falling into old patterns, and to change the programme.

For example, instead of saying to ourselves, 'my new partner is wonderful but they'll probably end up treating me badly just like all the others', we can insist that they're *not* any of the people we've been with before and there's no reason for them to behave in the same way – because this is a fresh start. But of course this must be accompanied by a genuine belief that we *deserve* a proper loving partner, which must over-ride any old subconscious beliefs, otherwise we will just attract another partner who'll be only too happy to demonstrate that these beliefs still exist within us.

It is the same if we've had a string of jobs that have gone badly, or with any other situation where we want to break the chain and change the programme.

The following piece of advice is therefore absolutely key to a life of abundance:

Our 'past' can only affect us if we choose to let it – and we can recreate ourselves afresh in each new moment of now, if we so choose.

the law of attraction

WHAT JESUS WAS REALLY SAYING

'Then pay attention to how you listen; for to those who have, more will be given; and from those who do not have, even what they seem to have will be taken away.' (Luke 8:18)

Again this simple passage has caused much confusion, but its message couldn't be much clearer to those who understand how our reality operates. It describes exactly how the law of attraction works.

We all know successful people who always seem to attract yet more success. If they have plenty of money they seem to attract even more. If they have plenty of friends they seem to attract even more. If they have plenty of respect and acclaim in their chosen field of work they seem to attract even more.

In the same way, we all know people who are always bemoaning their luck who tend to suffer ever more misfortune. It seems to stick to them like glue. Except it isn't misfortune at all – it's what they're *attracting* via their thoughts, preconceptions and beliefs.

So if we find ourselves more in the latter category than the former, it will be time for us to make some changes. We have seen that we need to develop our observer self, whose job is to spot when limiting beliefs are driving our thoughts and actions. We have also seen that we can break the chains of past patterns of behaviour, and make new, better choices.

Apart from these things, what other practical steps can we take to improve our experience? The simplest and most effective piece of advice is to stop allowing our everyday thoughts to fixate on the things we *don't* want in our life, and to focus instead on what we *do* want. This one aspect of manifesting what we desire in our life will keep our observer self extremely busy. But, if rigorously applied, it'll produce huge results all by itself.

What do we mean by focus? It means putting our whole self into visualising and affirming the person we want to be, or the outcomes we want to create. It means using our imagination and our emotions as much as possible to breathe life into our incipient creation. We have already seen that those who express their belief to the maximum act as if they've *already achieved* the outcome they desire.

If we recall how focused sportspeople are on their goals, often over a lengthy period, we need to be prepared to use that kind of dedication too if something is important enough to us. The fictional Dr Frankenstein was completely

WHAT ~~JESUS~~ FRANKENSTEIN WAS REALLY SAYING!

obsessed with creating life, and we can be the same except this time it's *our own*.

It is also the case that a true master can alter their reality in an instant – and this means *any* of us if we have sufficient belief.

However these observations come with a health warning. It doesn't hurt most of us to accept that our creations may take a little time to materialise. This means we need to stay excited and focused, yet loose, relaxed and patient. If we are over-expectant and impatient we tighten up on our dreams, our belief weakens and we let fear of not achieving them get in the way.

Some people perceive the pursuit of abundance as anathema to Jesus' original message of selfless love. But actually the two aren't in conflict at all.

WHAT JESUS WAS REALLY SAYING

First, our shared experience with the rest of humanity is *not* a competition, however much it might appear that way when we look, for example, at the apparent inequalities of resources and opportunities around our globe. All the evidence suggests that our individual and collective desires have the ability to manifest unlimited joyful abundance *for everyone* in our reality, because that's how it works. So if we're creating abundance for ourselves, it doesn't *have* to mean we're taking it away from someone else.

Second, the goal of creating joyful abundance for ourselves can be expressed in many ways. Some people may want to pursue what others would deride as unduly selfish or materialistic aims – such as having more money, a bigger house or a better body. But these are absolutely fine as long as they bring genuine happiness and joy to those who pursue them, and to the people around them. That is why the key is *joyful* abundance – because all too often the pursuit of purely materialist aims brings no joy, only an eternally unfulfilled yearning for more.

But we should be clear that, contrary to many orthodox religious worldviews, we're having this experience to *enjoy* it and to make the most of it. What is more there's *no one* in a position of supposed authority, in *any* realm, who'll judge us for whatever way we choose to express that. The only rider to this is that if at the same time we cause harm to someone else, especially knowingly and deliberately, our actions are no longer entirely love-based and expansive.

Other people may find happiness and joy in quite different ways, such as pursuing hobbies or sports and so on, and of course this is equally valid.

Having said that, precisely because love is such a strong motivator in this universe we're experiencing, some people feel strongly drawn to putting others before themselves – and this is their main source of pleasure. They might simply devote themselves to their family, or to their local community, or even to the wider global community in some way.

These are truly noble ideals – as long as they don't see themselves as in any way superior to those who don't choose that path, and as long as there's no tendency towards martyrdom. As we saw earlier, helping others with joy, not as a duty, is the only way to truly express love for them. What is more it's usually the case that, if concerns about global issues such as the environment are more driven by fear and anger than by love, over time this will have a seriously detrimental effect on the individuals involved.

anyone can do what he did

> *'I tell you, the one who believes in me will also do the works that I do and, in fact, will do greater works than these.' (John 14:11-12)*

We opened with the above quote, but it bears repeating because it tells us everything we need to know about just who we are. All the evidence suggests that with sufficient belief anyone, and that truly means *anyone*, can do what Jesus did.

Of course what's been handed down is that he only exhorted his closest followers to go out and follow his example:

> *Then Jesus called the twelve together and gave them power and authority over all demons and to cure diseases, and he sent them out to proclaim the kingdom of God... They departed and went through the villages, bringing the good news*

and curing diseases everywhere. (Luke 9:1-6)

The problem is that the Church fathers almost certainly tried to make out there was something special about these twelve, something that set them apart from the common man – just as they did to an even greater extent with Jesus himself.

But in truth we know full well that they were ordinary people – fishermen, tax collectors and so on. The only potential difference was their level of belief – and even that, as we saw earlier, was hardly perfect. They were human beings, just like us.

What is more it's highly likely that Jesus didn't just teach twelve people that they could to do what he did. That would've been unduly restrictive and, above all, elitist – and we might safely assume that elitism is the one thing that would've been genuinely abhorrent to him, even if the Church established in his name would go on to make it fundamental to their hierarchic structure.

Nor is it likely that he taught alone. Modern research stresses, for example, the hugely important part Mary Magdalene played in Jesus' mission – to the extent that she may even have been just as adept at manipulating reality as he was, except her work has been airbrushed from the records. What is more the two of them probably worked *closely* with many more than just twelve people.

But from a broader perspective Jesus and his followers showed thousands of people that they could manipulate their reality. Every time he allowed others to use him as a catalyst for their spiritual healing, often in front of large crowds, he was potentially trying to teach everyone there about the extent to which their belief could change their lives for the better.

We cannot know of the extent to which the people present misinterpreted this as Jesus being a special emissary of God working miracles no one else could perform, or whether these distortions only came into play subsequently. What we can surmise is that, in the unstable religious and political climate of the time, his public pronouncements would have to have remained relatively measured, possibly even partly obscured, for a reasonable length of time.

In fact there are repeated passages in the gospels where he's recorded as exhorting people to remain silent about what they'd seen. But if, rather than proclaiming himself the Son of God as the gospels would have us believe, he was actually telling them that they *themselves* were in control of their *own* destiny, rather than their religious and political leaders, we can see why. Making that known in a widespread and public way would've been entirely subversive and dangerous to the authorities, and would've got him arrested instantly – terminating his work before he'd been able to get his message out to a significant mass of people.

So it may indeed have been the case that his public pronouncements were for some time couched in veiled terms about, for example, the 'good news' of the kingdom of God or of heaven. But underneath this his intention would surely have been to let all who heard his message know that *within themselves* lay the keys that would unlock the illusion, eliminate suffering and lead to a life of joyful abundance:

WHAT JESUS WAS REALLY SAYING

'The kingdom of God is not coming with things that can be observed; nor will they say, "Look, here it is!" or "There it is!" For, in fact, the kingdom of God is within you.' (Luke 17:20-21)

Almost certainly he would've indicated that these keys are given to *everyone* as their birthright. To support this, several passages suggest strongly that his teachings were *not* reserved for any sort of elite, and didn't require any special knowledge or supposed wisdom:

'I tell you that many prophets and kings desired to see what you see, but did not see it, and to hear what you hear, but did not hear it.' (Luke 10:24)

'I thank you, Father, Lord of heaven and earth, because you have hidden these things from the wise and the intelligent and have revealed them

to infants.' (Matthew 11:25)

'Truly I tell you, unless you change and become like children, you will never enter the kingdom of heaven. Whoever becomes humble like this child is the greatest in the kingdom of heaven.' (Matthew 18:3-4)

It is also possible that his latter references to children were intended to emphasise that they tend to live absolutely in the moment, not worrying about the apparent past or future. This of course is exactly what allows anyone to break the chains of past associations, and to recreate themselves afresh in each new moment of now, if they so choose.

being the

light

WHAT JESUS WAS REALLY SAYING

Again Jesus spoke to them, saying, 'I am the light of the world. Whoever follows me will never walk in darkness but will have the light of life.' (John 8:12)

So we come to the end of our journey. It should be clear by now that this 'light of life' is almost certainly the knowledge of the illusion that masks our reality, and of the power over our own creations that we all possess. Once we recognise this the next step is to learn to use it consciously and deliberately, rather than unconsciously, in order to *follow our bliss*.

In doing this we can't help but illuminate the lives of others. By our example we'll automatically be spreading the 'good news', as Jesus and his followers tried to do so long ago. What is more we don't have to perform amazing feats – the example we set can be much simpler and more mundane than that.

Let us say we experience a setback of some kind – our partner or spouse leaves us, we lose our job, that sort of thing. What if we let the people around us see we're not suffering? What if we let them see us still taking responsibility, rather than blaming others? What if we let them see us refusing to fall into the trap of victimhood, but instead standing firm and strong and controlling our reaction? What if we even let them see us working out how we attracted that situation, and perhaps unearthing any 'silver lining' – even being able to do this *at the time* rather than months or years later?

Finally, what if we let them see us dust ourselves down and push on again, still creating a life of joyful abundance for ourselves and those around us? If we do that then maybe, when they're ready, they'll start to think: 'Perhaps there's something in this I need to understand better?' We can present those close to us with no finer gift.

It is important to understand that the foregoing example isn't one of stoicism, or fortitude in the face of some sort of inevitable adversity or even fate. It is much more proactive than that. It's taking *control* of our life with *dynamism* and *energy*.

We have seen that, unfortunately, many of us spend much of our time suffering and in victim mode – or even just 'surviving' life. As experiences go these are perfectly valid choices. But that's not what we're really here for:

Life isn't about suffering, or mere survival. We expand the consciousness of our divine supersoul far more if we aim for joyful abundance and to fulfil our maximum potential – subject to any constraints imposed by our birth givens or other challenges we've collected along the way.

In our modern world differently-abled athletes, or those who face severe illness with bravery and selflessness, are a shining example – and there are many others if we look around us.

Jesus told us that we *are* the light, and that we should always strive to be it:

> *'You are the light of the world. A city built on a hill cannot be hidden. No one after lighting a lamp puts it under the bushel basket, but on the lamp stand, and it gives light to all in the house. In the same way, let your light shine before others, so that they may see your good works.' (Matthew 5:14-16)*

Let us hope that this time many more of us are ready to learn from what he had to tell us, to heed his advice – and to truly *live*.

WHAT JESUS WAS REALLY SAYING

The following are the major miracles referred to in this book. The account quoted is in italics, but it can clearly be seen that most of them appear in more than one gospel:

	Matthew	Mark	Luke	John
Time in the wilderness	*4:1-2*	1:12-13	4:1-13	
Turning water into wine				*2:1-11*
Feeding the 5000	*14:14-21*	6:32-44	9:11-17	6:1-13
Sudden haul of fish			*5:3-7*	
Stilling the storm	*8:23-27*	4:35-41	8:22-25	
Walking on water	*14:23-31*	6:45-52		
Disciples forget bread	16:5-12	*8:14-21*		
Transfiguration into light body	*17:1*	9:2-8	9:28-36	
Empty tomb	*28:1-8*	16:1-8	24:1-12	20:1-13
Appearance after death	*28:9-10*	*16:9-14*	24:13-53	20:14-31

also by the author

all published by Rational Spirituality Press
www.rspress.org

Note that all books published from 2013 on reflect the more state-of-the-art worldview of 'Supersoul Spirituality', those before the more traditional 'Rational Spirituality'. See ianlawton.com for more details.

RESEARCH BOOKS

AFTERLIFE (2016) is a state-of-the-art, clear, reliable guide to the afterlife based on the underlying consistencies in modern out-of-body research.

THE POWER OF YOU (2014) compares modern channelled wisdom from Seth, Abraham and others, all emphasising that each of us is consciously creating every aspect of our own reality, and that this is what the current consciousness shift is all about.

SUPERSOUL (2013) is the main reference book for Supersoul Spirituality, containing out-of-body and other evidence that each and every one of us is a holographic reflection of a supersoul that has power way beyond our wildest imaginings.

THE HISTORY OF THE SOUL (2010) reinterprets

the most revered ancient texts and traditions from all around the world about a forgotten golden race that became debased and was wiped out in a catastrophe.

THE BIG BOOK OF THE SOUL (2008) is the main reference book for Rational Spirituality, containing full details of key cases, in-depth analysis of all key topics and full source references.

THE WISDOM OF THE SOUL (2007) contains the results of a new style of research that attempts to answer a number of key universal questions by regressing ten subjects into the interlife.

SIMPLE BOOKS

SHIT DOESN'T JUST HAPPEN!! (2016) introduces Supersoul Spirituality by explaining how and why we ourselves create or attract everything we experience in our adult lives… so that we are never victims of chance, God's will, our karma or our life plans.

THE GIFT (2013) describes the three timeless treasures of transformation – inner peace, conscious creation and being love – and how to use the sword of love to cut off your worst fears at source.

THE FUTURE OF THE SOUL (2010) contains crucial channelled messages about 2012 and the global shift in consciousness.

YOUR HOLOGRAPHIC SOUL (2010) uses a question-and-answer style. It tackles seven key questions to build a Rational Spiritual framework, and then offers ten self-help suggestions for how we can use it to get the most out of our lives.

THE LITTLE BOOK OF THE SOUL (2007) uses a story-book style. It contains a selection of the most interesting near-death and past-life cases that support Rational Spirituality, interspersed with simple summaries and analysis.

[These last three are also available in the large format trilogy AN INTRODUCTION TO THE SOUL.]

SPIRITUAL NOVELS

THE GIRL WHO LEARNED TO LIVE (2012) is the moving story of a disadvantaged girl's search for love and fulfilment, and the secrets she uncovers along the way.

THE MAN WHO DIDN'T DIE (2011) is a gripping novel about how a successful businessman's life changes after he kills his beloved wife in a car crash, and finds himself paralysed from the neck down.

IAN LAWTON was born in 1959. Formerly an accountant, sales exec, business and IT consultant and avid bike and car racer, in his mid-thirties he changed tack completely to become a writer-researcher specialising in ancient history and, more recently, spiritual philosophy. His first two books, *Giza: The Truth* and *Genesis Unveiled*, sold over 30,000 copies worldwide.

In his non-fiction *Books of the Soul* series he has developed the ideas of Rational Spirituality and of the holographic soul, while most recently he has introduced the radical concept of the supersoul. Short film clips discussing all these can be found at *www.ianlawton.com* and on YouTube.

Lightning Source UK Ltd.
Milton Keynes UK
UKOW06f1910190116

266720UK00015B/369/P

9 780992 816315